100 QUESTIONS

Black People

Should Ask Themselves

_____

A Candid Conversation

by
John Hall & J. D. Smith

Introduction

This book is for black people.

I want to be abundantly clear that I am not anti-white, anti-police, or anti-government. Martin Luther King Jr. believed that we should be judged by the content of our character. I love black people. I love white people. I love ALL people. I love America. My father was an Illinois State Police officer for 30 years. Many of my family members are current or former police officers and military service members.

I decided to write this book, because there are a multitude of issues in America that specifically affect black people. My goal is to help facilitate a necessary conversation within the black community — a conversation that will lead us to look inside of ourselves and make the positive changes necessary for a successful future as black Americans.

Black people have always had a complicated relationship with America. We helped build this great nation; however, there are countless instances where our progress and very existence has been undermined. From Jim Crow, to redlining, to for-profit prisons that unfairly and disproportionately incarcerate minorities, the American ideal that all men are created equal has not been a freedom afforded to black Americans throughout our history. The evidence of historic, prolonged, and consistent institutional racism makes it abundantly clear that black people must take personal responsibility for accelerating our own success within our communities and culture. One thing we do very well as individuals, is overcome adversity. One thing we do poorly as a community, is truly support one another. This is essential in order to thrive collectively.

The black community can build a better America for itself once we collectively acknowledge that it is solely our responsibility to implement the changes necessary to do so. We need more black Americans working in government, technology, law enforcement, and legal professions. Above all, in order to prosper, we need to cultivate real love for one another.

It is my hope that this book is shared in barber shops, hair salons, churches, coffee shops, on college campuses, and at family dinners. Beginning a conversation that facilitates inward reflection within the black community is imperative in order to collectively come to the understanding that we need to invest in ourselves.

John Hall
Founder of Wealth Legion

"CHANGE WILL NOT COME IF WE WAIT FOR SOME OTHER PERSON OR SOME OTHER TIME. WE ARE THE ONES WE'VE BEEN WAITING FOR. WE ARE THE CHANGE THAT WE SEEK."

- President Barack Obama

QUESTION #1

Where do you want to be in 10 years?

QUESTION #2

For how many generations back do you
know the names of your ancestors?

QUESTION #3

Do you know how to calculate your net worth?

John Hall

QUESTION #4

What is preventing you from
maintaining an emergency fund?

John Hall

QUESTION #5

Do you discuss finances and
wealth strategies at the dinner table?

John Hall

QUESTION #6

Are you and your family members
adequately covered with life insurance?

John Hall

QUESTION #7

Have you prepared your will?

QUESTION #8

Why is it socially acceptable to
kill black people?

John Hall

QUESTION #9

Who was the most impactful
historical black figure?

John Hall

QUESTION #10

What hinders the
creation of economically
successful black communities?

John Hall

QUESTION #11

What limiting beliefs do we hold that prevent us from progressing culturally, and socioeconomically?

John Hall

QUESTION #12

For you personally, how important is it to
see more black people succeed in life?

John Hall

QUESTION #13

What is your trusted source for financial advice and education?

John Hall

QUESTION #14

What personal choices prevent
you from actively
participating in building a better
future for black Americans?

John Hall

QUESTION #15

Do you regularly consider how your individual actions impact the status of black people in America?

John Hall

QUESTION #16

What positive results could come from black
communities supporting each
other in the same way that
immigrant communities "take
care of their own"?

John Hall

QUESTION #17

What is the greatest challenge that all black people face for which we cannot blame anyone but ourselves?

John Hall

QUESTION #18

What progress have we made in America since the civil rights movement?

John Hall

QUESTION #19

In recent years, what positive results have come from marching in the streets for civil justice and social change?

QUESTION #20

How can we defeat the crabs in a barrel syndrome in our neighborhoods?

John Hall

QUESTION #21

What are the biggest advantages of being African American?

John Hall

QUESTION #22

How do you feel about the terms
"African American" and "black people"?

John Hall

QUESTION #23

Do you think there are sufficient news outlets covering topics that are important and relevant to black people?

John Hall

QUESTION #24

Why do we glorify the accomplishments of athletes and celebrities more than commonplace professional occupations?

John Hall

QUESTION #25

When voting, do you select candidates
who work to affect black interests?

John Hall

QUESTION #26

What actions will you take to protect black women and children?

John Hall

QUESTION #27

With frequent news featuring unarmed people of color being killed, why have we not established a coordinated system and effort to affect real change to stop these killings?

John Hall

QUESTION #28

What ideas do you have that could improve conditions for black people that you are willing and able to act upon?

QUESTION #29

Why do we criticize the efforts of
our fellow brothers and sisters
who are trying to do something positive?

John Hall

QUESTION #30

What is the black woman's greatest
contribution to society?

John Hall

QUESTION #31

What can you do to avoid
hurting black women?

QUESTION #32

What is the black man's greatest contribution to society?

John Hall

QUESTION #33

Do you lack trust in black men? If so, why?

John Hall

QUESTION #34

Why haven't you visited Africa yet?

John Hall

QUESTION #35

How have rap and hip-hop culture
contributed to the overall
well-being of black people?

John Hall

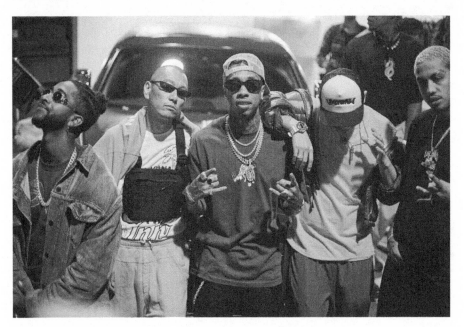

QUESTION #36

Would dressing in classy attire
that projects self-respect contribute
more positively to society's image
of black people?

John Hall

QUESTION #37

What can we do individually to diminish,
and ultimately eradicate,
negative black stereotypes?

QUESTION #38

Which customs from our history
should be kept and which customs
are no longer serving us?

John Hall

QUESTION #39

Do you feel that minorities receive fair representation in roles and are awarded equitably for their work in Hollywood?

John Hall

QUESTION #40

Overall, how has affirmative action
helped or hurt minorities?

QUESTION #41

Aside from the industries of sports and entertainment, what major positive contributions are black people making to America?

QUESTION #42

What feelings do you believe
society has toward black people?

QUESTION #43

If you had all the money you would ever need, what would you do with your life?

John Hall

QUESTION #44

What professions do we encourage
black children to pursue?

John Hall

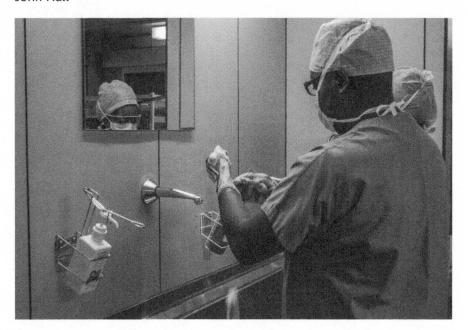

QUESTION #45

Do you feel respected by your boss and that
your work is valued by your company?

John Hall

QUESTION #46

What impact does a long commute
have on your quality of life?

John Hall

QUESTION #47

Why haven't you written the book you
said you wanted to create?

John Hall

QUESTION #48

How could continuous self-education
and a consistent habit of
reading benefit you?

QUESTION #49

What steps have you taken to create the invention you thought of?

John Hall

QUESTION #50

How important to you is access to quality healthcare?

John Hall

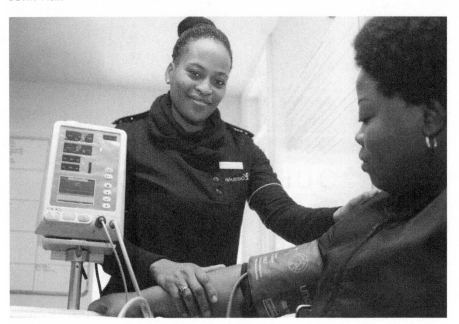

QUESTION #51

What will you do if you are
displaced by gentrification?

QUESTION #52

How often do you travel to see new places?

QUESTION #53

What is your approach to cultivating and maintaining positive mental health?

John Hall

QUESTION #54

What can an individual do to overcome a
reliance on government benefits?

John Hall

QUESTION #55

Are you willing to commit to uplifting others instead of criticizing their efforts?

QUESTION #56

How many books have you
voluntarily read since high school?

John Hall

QUESTION #57

What kind of business could you start
with your family members?

John Hall

QUESTION #58

How important is it to recirculate your dollars within your own community?

QUESTION #59

Why do you buy brands that have a
history of disrespecting us?

QUESTION #60

How do we develop a solid infrastructure in economically depressed communities?

John Hall

QUESTION #61

Why haven't you developed the product you always dreamed of creating?

QUESTION #62

Would you be willing to invest time
to research opportunities that will bring in
money by leveraging the efforts of others?

John Hall

QUESTION #63

What is your knowledge of the tax advantages and other benefits that accompany small business ownership?

John Hall

QUESTION #64

Why do we continually accrue debt instead
of committing to accumulate assets?

John Hall

QUESTION #65

Why do we continually try to fit in
corporate America instead of starting
our own small businesses and
creating jobs that can employ people of color?

QUESTION #66

If you haven't already, when will you begin investing in the stock market?

John Hall

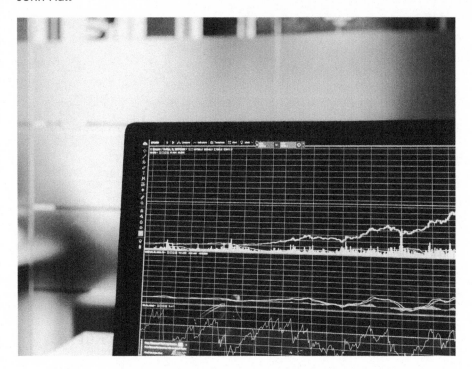

QUESTION #67

How could you benefit from
hiring a financial coach?

John Hall

QUESTION #68

Does your household have more money invested in Jordans than in stocks?

QUESTION #69

What can be done to eliminate the plague
of gun violence that devastates
our communities?

John Hall

QUESTION #70

How would the people who died in the
civil rights movement feel
about what's going
on in the black community today?

QUESTION #71

Who are your living heroes who are black
and what can we do to build upon
their legacies and accomplishments?

John Hall

QUESTION #72

How are politics used to affect
conditions for black people?

QUESTION #73

How can we create sustainable income opportunities in impoverished communities?

QUESTION #74

What steps can we take to
ensure healthier foods are
more accessible in black communities?

John Hall

QUESTION #75

What would motivate you to get more actively involved in politics and promote participation among your friends, family, and neighbors?

QUESTION #76

For damages suffered by the
legacy of slavery, do you believe
that awarding reparations to
the descendants of slaves is fair
recompense, and acknowledgement
of wrongdoing by the U.S. government?

John Hall

QUESTION #77

How much do you know about
the industry of for-profit prisons?

John Hall

QUESTION #78

How do you explain racism to your
children while also
helping them understand that
we must not foster reciprocal hate?

QUESTION #79

How does social media affect your life?

QUESTION #80

What support systems do you have
in place to ensure
success and overall wellness
in the following areas: emotional,
professional, financial, health, spir-
itual, family?

John Hall

QUESTION #81

How do you educate your children beyond the standard curriculum of the school system?

QUESTION #82

Can you name one black CEO that runs a publicly traded company?

QUESTION #83

Do you guide the direction of your
children's education on a
path that can advance your own
family's empire?

John Hall

QUESTION #84

Do you plan on enrolling your children
in a STEM summer program?

John Hall

QUESTION #85

Why is it common, in a
variety of situations, for a black
person to be treated negatively,
whereas other ethnic groups would be
treated more favorably?

QUESTION #86

What would it mean to you to have
on-call access with
an attorney who can speak
with authorities on your behalf in the
event you or a member of your
immediate family is racially profiled?

John Hall

QUESTION #87

What are your thoughts on
criminal justice reform and
the corruption within the justice system?

John Hall

QUESTION #88

Do you feel politicians and the government are going to
make things better for us,
or do we need to create a plan to make
things better for ourselves?

John Hall

QUESTION #89

What is the biggest hurdle black people
face in our society that is
seemingly beyond our control?

John Hall

QUESTION #90

What is necessary for a majority of black people to economically thrive in America?

John Hall

QUESTION #91

What would it mean to you to entrust your money in a black owned bank?

John Hall

QUESTION #92

How do we create large-scale
businesses that are the
employers of choice for blacks?

QUESTION #93

What are you willing to sacrifice to help build our global community of successful black people?

John Hall

QUESTION #94

Is it important for you to take a stand for the equality and freedom we deserve?

John Hall

QUESTION #95

What is the appropriate age to discuss with your children how to interact with police?

QUESTION #96

What is the definition of a black person?

John Hall

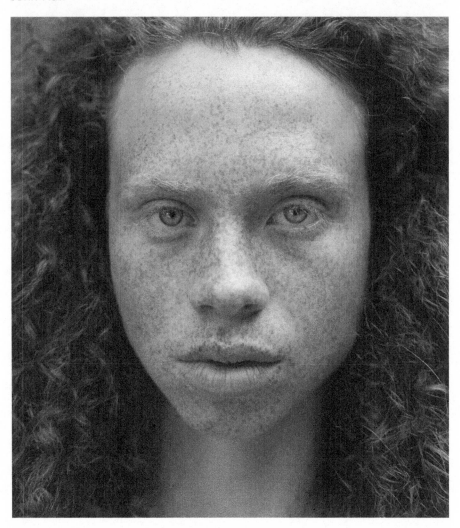

QUESTION #97

What progress and achievements would you like to see for black people during your lifetime?

John Hall

QUESTION #98

How do we create strong families?

QUESTION #99

At the end of your life, how do you
want to be remembered?

PSALM XXIII

THE LORD IS MY SHEPHERD:
I SHALL NOT WANT.

2 HE MAKETH ME TO LIE DOWN
IN GREEN PASTURES. HE LEADETH
ME BESIDE THE STILL WATERS.

3 HE RESTORETH MY SOUL: HE
LEADETH ME IN THE PATHS OF
RIGHTEOUSNESS FOR HIS NAME'S
SAKE.

4 YEA, THOUGH I WALK THROUGH
THE VALLEY OF THE SHADOW OF
DEATH, I WILL FEAR NO EVIL: FOR
THOU ART WITH ME; THY ROD AND
THY STAFF THEY COMFORT ME.

5 THOU PREPAREST A TABLE
BEFORE ME IN THE PRESENCE OF
MINE ENEMIES: THOU ANOINTEST
MY HEAD WITH OIL; MY CUP
RUNNETH OVER.

6 SURELY GOODNESS AND MERCY
SHALL FOLLOW ME ALL THE DAYS
OF MY LIFE: AND I WILL DWELL,
IN THE HOUSE OF THE LORD
FOR EVER.

QUESTION #100

What will be your greatest
contribution to the world?

Closing Statement

Dr. Martin Luther King Jr. had a vision that was rooted within a dream. For most black people this vision is still unrealized. The time has come for black people to come together and we want to create a bridge through thought provoking questions. I believe that questions are unheard answers. A question produces action in the mind, which leads to a physical result. By starting this conversation, we can form solutions to some of our most pressing problems.

Throughout my lifetime, I have seen failed efforts in areas of achieving racial justice, creating socioeconomic progress, and providing access to fair housing. Past efforts have taught us that the journey towards equality is a dilapidated, winding, treacherous path. Despite historical hurdles, we must tackle issues from the lack of adequate financial education, to overcoming our perpetual status as second-class citizens. We must create solutions today in order for future generations to thrive. It is important to have a clear collective vision, of which we must all take part in ownership, in order to achieve a better standing in society.

Taking self-responsibility allows one to focus on the pursuit of future success rather than the injustices of the past. We cannot control every factor that led to our current circumstances. The goal is to focus on what we can control and how we respond.

The opportunities to create a brighter future are right before us. The candid conversations necessary to identify and harness those opportunities can begin now. It is our job, today, to take the steps required to build that future.

The task of building a better future falls upon all of us. Now is the time for black Americans to bring more seats to the economic table. Oftentimes it can feel as though we have to ask permission to be black. Simply "being" has required some sort of outside approval and acceptance. It is time to accept ourselves and take the steps necessary to claim our rights to life, liberty, and the pursuit of happiness in America.

J.D. Smith
Founder - Hipturist.com

John Hall

Sources Cited (Rear Cover)

Data of incarceration rate of blacks.

NAACP.org
https://www.naacp.org/criminal-justice-fact-sheet/

Black Net Worth by 2053.

Charlene Rhinehart
'African American Wealth May Fall To Zero By 2053'
Black Enterprise
July 12th 2019
https://www.blackenterprise.com/african-american-wealth-zero-2053/

Americans Killed By Police.

The Washington Post
https://www.washingtonpost.com/graphics/2019/national/police-shootings-2019/?noredirect=on

Made in the USA
Monee, IL
05 June 2020